STENCILING

Stenciling

140 Historical Patterns
for Individual Decoration

Ilse Maierbacher

4880 Lower Valley Road, Atglen, PA 19310 USA

Copyright © 1997 by Schiffer Publishing, Ltd.
Library of Congress Catalog Card Number 97-80031

Translated by Dr. Edward Force,
Central Connecticul State University

Original 1995 German language edition published by
Georg D. W. Callwey, Munich, Germany.

ISBN: 0-7643-0376-7
Printed in China

Published by Schiffer Publishing Ltd.
4880 Lower Valley Road
Atglen, PA 19310
Phone: (610) 593-1777; Fax: (610) 593-2002
Please write for a free catalog.
This book may be purchased from the publisher.
Please include $3.95 for shipping.

Try your bookstore first.

We are interested in hearing from authors
with book ideas on related subjects.

Ilse Maierbacher

Ilse Maierbacher, works as a gilder and cask
painter in a German restoration shop. Roland Bunge
is a free-lance photographer for architecture and
monument preservation.

ACKNOWLEDGEMENTS
I extend my hearty thanks to Sabine-Beate
Lehnert and Reiner Neubauer for their friendly,
helpful support.

PHOTO CREDITS
All the pictures in this book were provided by
Roland Bunge of Dresden, except for #46 (Ger-
man Basket Museum, Michelau) and #49
(Franconian Open-air Museum, Bad Windsheim.

Stencil Archives:
Sabine-Beate Lehnert, Prien
Reiner Neubauer Restoration Shop, Bad Endorf
Reinhard Zehentner Collection, Mühldorf
Claudia Boelti, Rimsting
Ilse Maierbacher, Aschau

CONTENTS

1. This area shows four different uses of stencils—two different stencils were each used twice, each with differing brightness. The first one was reconstructed (see page 105).

2. During a reconstruction project, these stenciled decorations were discovered on ceilings and walls. Every decoration appears completely once, preserved for reconstruction.

3. This old wall was decorated several times, one on top of the other. The original color illustrates the tastes of the times (circa 1900), which made the room appear rather dark.

INTRODUCTION

Stenciling as a wall or room decoration is experiencing a vehement renaissance in Germany at this time.

Interest is great, though there is a lack of motif patterns. Many of the historic decorations were lost, victim to an attitude of disdain toward all things not modern following World War II, as well as to a lack of hand-crafting ability. Half a century later, though, there is a recognized demand for that which was once relegated to the past.

This book details a unique and extensive collection of historic stenciling decorations from the art's high-point of popularity in Germany, dating from before the turn of the century and lasting until 1940. For the most part, the 140 examples shown here are original stencils or were discovered during searches for materials.

The patterns here are primarily shown in their original colors, as noted in the photo captions. The choice of colors, to be sure, does not always correspond to present-day taste, and one may well want to choose colors to match their own personal tastes. There are no bounds for the imagination in this process.

In order to make the work enjoyable as well as successful, there is a thorough description of the hand-crafting process. There are varying degrees of difficulty among the stencils pictured to allow each person to find projects they feel confident with, from a single-colored frieze or a multicolored border with stripes to a decoration that fills the entire wall.

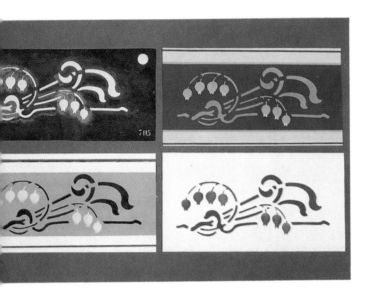

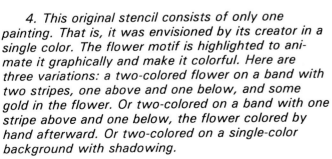

4. This original stencil consists of only one painting. That is, it was envisioned by its creator in a single color. The flower motif is highlighted to animate it graphically and make it colorful. Here are three variations: a two-colored flower on a band with two stripes, one above and one below, and some gold in the flower. Or two-colored on a band with one stripe above and one below, the flower colored by hand afterward. Or two-colored on a single-color background with shadowing.

5/6. Two more examples with shadowing, a technique that makes the frieze look more three-dimensional. Even the simple graphic frieze is enlivened by it. The shadow is first spotted in one color. It goes downward to the right (southeast).

HISTORY — A LOOK BACKWARD

Stenciling is not a new method of decorating — it's an age-old handicraft. From ancient days to the present, it has seen widespread use in Asia, America, and Europe, on walls, containers, and textiles. Now as then, stenciling is a tried-and-true means of applying repeating patterns much faster than by painting them freehand, and also of making them much more uniform than would be possible in freehand work.

New technology that made paint more available and affordable in the nineteenth century resulted in a blossoming of painted decorations in secular buildings. For example, until about 1840, genuine ultramarine paint could only be produced through an expensive, labor-intensive process from the semiprecious stone, lapis lazuli. Once breakthroughs came to produce it artificially, luxuriant blue designs quickly appeared on walls and ceilings. A real wealth of color began to appear in bourgeois houses, and a new occupation came into being. The decorative painter practiced a handicraft that no longer exists in Germany, and that can best be compared with that of the church painter. Training for this occupation can still be acquired in Bavaria.

Stenciling is one aspect of decoration painting. Often whole walls and even ceiling surfaces are decorated with patterns.

Usually several painters work on one job because stencils made of oiled or painted cardboard are unwieldy in size — between 50 and 70 centimeters wide, and sometimes more, depending on the type of pattern. One person holds the stencil on the wall, and his colleague applies the paint.

The most commonly used technique is called spotting. For this, a round brush with short, stiff bristles is dipped in paint then tapped against the walls perpendicularly, in hammer-like movements. The old works demonstrate that, then as now, time was money. Even then, work was done very quickly. Spots were left where they fell, and the stencils sometimes slipped.

7. Elaborate ceiling and wall decorations with many stripes were used, particularly in houses of the upper bourgeoisie. This room in an inn shows a reconstruction based on the original. In addition, another painting technique adorns the space — marbling on the ceiling and window area.

Painters designed the decorations and cut the stencils themselves at the beginning of bourgeois art's stenciling era, but, industrial production of these tools developed around the turn of the century. Stencils were often supplied along with color charts that made it easier for the painter to choose harmonious colors for multicolored friezes. The decoration's form and the combination of colors are equally important to the overall appearance.

8. A factory-stamped original stencil of cardboard with a number and the added "GES. GESCH:" (protected by law). On page 7 it is shown twice with shadowing.

The stencils were numbered, and some of them were even copyrighted. Traveling salesmen helped distribute equipment to German painters and there were advertisements in the trade paper *Die Mappe—Deutsche Malerzeitschrift*.

This presumed simplification of their art bothered many painters at the time, though there was no stopping it. Today the same decoration can be found in Cologne as in Dresden.

Stenciling was not completely without controversy. Ludwig Reisberger, who was the editor of *Die Mappe—Deutsche Malerzeitschrift* in the 1920s, advocated freehand painting for friezes.

He engaged in an ongoing debate with the Union of German Painting Stencil Manufacturers over several issues. One reader even described these manufacturers as the "gravediggers of the painters' handicraft."

Despite all negative prognoses, things did not go that far. The painters' handicraft still exists, and the stenciling is enjoying its second high point at this time. It not only offers hobbyists a field for their imaginations, but provides professional painters with new/old decorating techniques to enrich their work.

9. An advertisement from Die Mappe—Deutsche Malerzeitung, 1924. One of many advertisements from one of many stencil manufacturers.

PART I
MATERIALS AND TECHNIQUES

Backgrounds

Before choosing a decoration, such as a frieze, one must determine whether the background is suitable. In the past, more or less smoothly polished walls, as well as surfaces with a small-grained surface structure and wooden walls served as backgrounds.

Smooth or fine-grained surfaces remain the ideal backgrounds to this day. On rough surfaces, the patterns will vary, which seldom looks good. Rough fiber is suitable, to be sure, but it does not allow any really sharp contours. Wallpaper without any relief structure is only suitable when it is glued on so firmly that it can take two coats of paint for the background.

Embossed, vinyl, textile, and other wallpapers must be removed, which usually requires small- or large-scale cleaning and plastering afterward.

The wall paints available today—dispersion and mineral paints—are suitable as backgrounds for full-tone, poster, and acrylic paints to spot-paint the pattern.

One can also mix powdered pigments in various binding agents and thus produce the paints oneself. But this is comparatively expensive and better suited to the professional painter, who has these pigments on hand anyway. Paints made with powdered pigments are also unbeatable in terms of their glowing color.

10/11. The same stencil pattern is shown on smooth and rough backgrounds for comparison. On a rough surface, no sharp contours are possible. Yet the result is impressive. Less detailed decorations are even better suited to rough surfaces. Pages 100 and 101 show a use of this design.

THE STENCIL

There are two types of stencil: the one-stroke, single-colored stencils and the multi-stroke, multicolored stencils. Each color has its own application, its own stencil.

SINGLE-COLORED

The single-colored stencil is intended for a single-colored frieze. It is applied end to end, duplicating itself. The orientation points are the "locating marks," holes specially stamped into the stencil for locating and forming either part of the decoration or additional spots that are painted over afterward. Parts of the decorations can also be locating marks. Naturally, they are not painted over.

There are also stencils that are located without locating marks. So that this can be done as precisely as possible, locators are often in the longest part of the decoration.

MULTICOLORED

With multicolored stencils, friezes of two or more colors are painted. Thus the first pattern is applied followed by another until the beginning and end of the pattern meet. Then a second, overlaying pattern is applied on top for a different color, and thus it goes on, each passage in a different color. As locating points for the following strokes, the locating marks are once again used, consisting of either dots or parts of the decoration.

12. In the upper stencil, the dots (pointed out with arrows) serve as locating marks. They are integrated into the decoration. In the lower illustration, parts of the decoration serve as locating marks. They become part of the finished frieze.

13. A frieze without locating marks (see page 46). It was simply placed and painted. This requires great precision in one's work, so that no splitting or overlapping results.

14. A two-color design: showing the first coat, the second coat, and the complete frieze. →

The overlapping stencil is for multicolored designs. The individual strokes more or less overlay each other, so that once they are completed, the contours of the individual strokes cannot always be recognized clearly. There are drawings for these stencils in Part II.

In overlapping strokes, the sequence of stencils and colors is obligatory, as outlined in the captions. Any variation in sequence would change and most likely ruin the decoration.

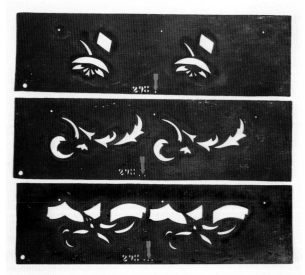

15. An original stencil for three colors was manufactured with two designs stamped next to each other. The number of holes behind the number (note the arrows) indicates the painting sequence. Any change would damage or even ruin the appearance. (This is true only of overlapping stencils.)

16. An illustration of the individual colors and, at the bottom, all three combined as a finished design with just one pattern. (The design in color is shown on page 57.)

The precision of the locating marks helps to assure the success of the work. This is even more important with multicolored stencils than with single-colored ones (see illustration #16).

A characteristic feature of the stencil is the bridges. They are uncut areas left out of the pattern to prevent the stencil from coming apart or giving way during painting. Like locating marks, bridges were sometimes painted over afterward, sometimes with special stencils for just such a purpose. Usually, though, these bridges were constructed to became part of the whole decoration (see #17).

17. Opposite page, top: In this Art Nouveau stencil, the arrows point out the bridges that hold the whole stencil together and prevent the long, thin, and thus unstable arches from flexing (which would distort the shapes). The bridges are located so that they fit harmoniously into the design, even giving it its characteristic appearance. (Page 109 shows a space decorated with this design.)

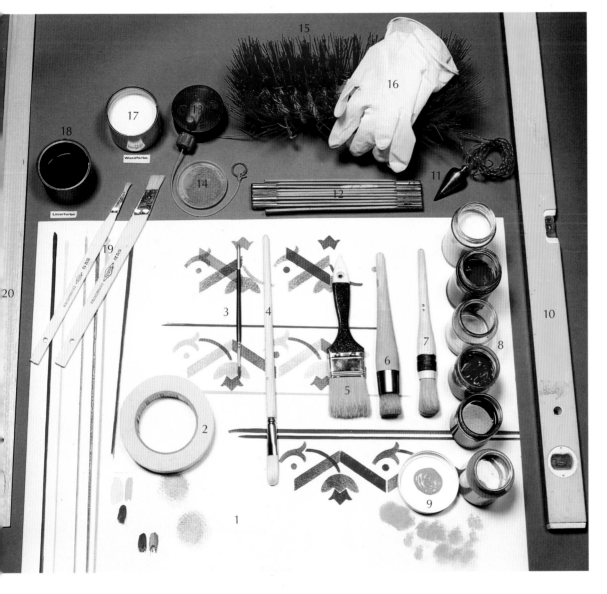

18. Tools and materials for stencil painting, striping and spattering:

1. Multipurpose cardboard sheet, for stenciling and striping practice, testing color, and wiping brushes.
2. Masking tape for various uses.
3-4. Pointed brush and small bristle brush for retouching and background improvements.
5. Paintbrush for graining technique, stripes, and stencil painting (cardboard).
6. Spotting brush, available in various sizes.
7. Round, soft stenciling brush for hatching technique.
8. Several stencil paints.
9. Plate for small amounts of paint.
10. Spirit level and
11. Plumb line, used for wall-filling stencils.
12. Folding rule.
13. Chalk line for marking lines on the wall.
14. Light chalk powder to fill chalk-line box.
15. Brush and
16. Rubber glove for spattering.
17. Background paint (wall paint).
18. Striping paint, somewhat more liquid than stenciling paint.
19. Two striping brushes of different widths for painting different sizes of stripes.
20. Wooden ruler for striping.

Tools and Materials

19. Tools and materials for making stencils:
1. Firm composition board with pressed wood on one side and Formica on the other for cutting and stamping.
2. Hammer.
3. Punches with different diameters.
4. Stencil-cutting knife.
5. Pencil.
6. Eraser.
7. Drawing triangle.
8. Scissors.
9. Metal ruler with beveled edge.
10. Mylar or Acetate.
11. Photocopy of the design.
12. Carbon paper.
13. Stencil cardboard (0.3-0.5 millimeters thick).
14. Lacquer for the cardboard.
15. Paintbrush.

Making
Stencils

The size of the decorations in this book can be altered with the help of a photocopier. The size of the stenciled decoration should harmonize with the proportions of the room where it will be used.

I advise you to photocopy your chosen design in various sizes and to experiment, attaching them to the wall and observing them from a distance.

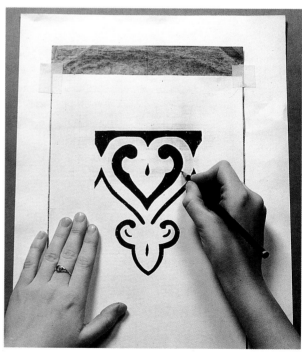

20. Making a cardboard stencil: Carbon paper is placed between cardboard and photocopy, and held with tape to prevent slipping. The lines are drawn carefully with a sharp pencil.

CARDBOARD STENCILS

Use carbon paper and a sharp pencil to copy the decoration from the photocopy to cardboard, which should be about 0.3 millimeters thick. If the cardboard is too thick, the painted designs will appear somewhat smaller and the finer details will not reproduce well.

For every color, a separate stencil must be cut using a stencil-cutting knife.

Suitable surfaces to cut on include firm cardboard, pressed board, rigid plastic, and wood. When cutting, be careful that the pencil mark is cut away, otherwise the design will unintentionally become smaller. Holes can be made with a stamping iron. For this, a hard surface underneath is necessary—Formica and similar hard, smooth, artificial materials are well suited.

The finished stencil should be protected with a coat of paint. A quick drying rust-proofing paint made for metal, often works. This paint dries very quickly, so that the required four coats on the front and back can be applied within a short time. However, any kind of thin liquid paint that one has at home can also be used. Drying time will be indicated on the can. Once it has four coats, a cardboard stencil is resistant enough to be used for a frieze in at least two rooms.

MYLAR/ACETATE STENCILS

This material is stronger, can be cleaned more often, and is therefore better suited for wall-filling stencils. Since small openings fill up quickly, regular cleanings are important for filigree patterns. The material should be between 1/3 and 1/2 millimeter thick and should be stored flat. (Mylar and Acetate that are kept on a roll don't lose their curvature and curl up when used, resulting in inaccurate designs.) Since the foil is transparent, one can place it over the photocopied design and draw the contours on with a sharp pencil.

The same surfaces used for cutting cardboard are suitable for cutting the plastic. But holes can only be stamped on very firm surfaces: Formica or other rigid, smooth plastics. It is best to go to a lumber dealer and get a leftover piece of Formica paneling, which has a hard surface of pressed material on one side and smooth wood on the other. You can use this to cut and stamp both kinds of stencil materials.

21. To make a stencil with Mylar or Acetate, place the plastic on top of the photocopy and precisely draw the lines with a sharp pencil.

22. The cardboard or foil is placed on a hard surface and cut out with a sharp knife. The pencil lines are cut away too, otherwise the design parts would be too small and the spaces in between too big.

23. Holes for the locating marks and small round spots (see photo) in the design can be cut easily, quickly and precisely with stamping tools. Foil requires a very hard base under it. Formica or a similar hard, smooth material is especially suitable.

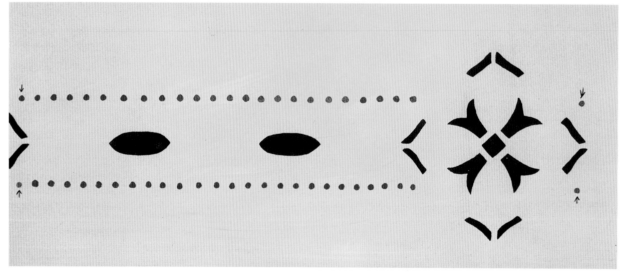

For very small designs, two or three sequential colors can be kept on one stencil, if it is practical. If the design's different colors are spaced apart, the complete decoration can be cut on one stencil. If necessary, the second color area can be covered with masking tape while the first color is being painted.

24. This original stencil shows three designs in a row. With a total length of 62 centimeters, it is not easy to use. But a smaller design can be repeated numerous times if it is not longer than 35 to 40 centimeters. That is a handy size.

25. This was originally a single-color stencil. But the parts of the design are so far apart that one can also paint it in two colors.

26. A five-piece original stencil with remains of the paint used. (See color pictures on pages 2 and 83.)

27. A three-piece original stencil (shown on Page 70)

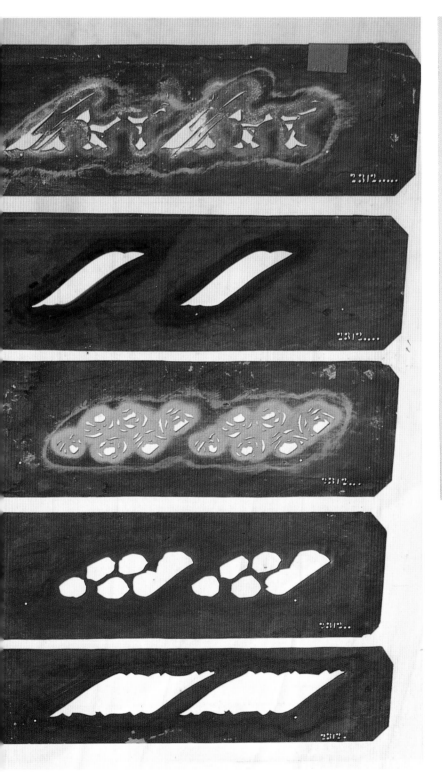

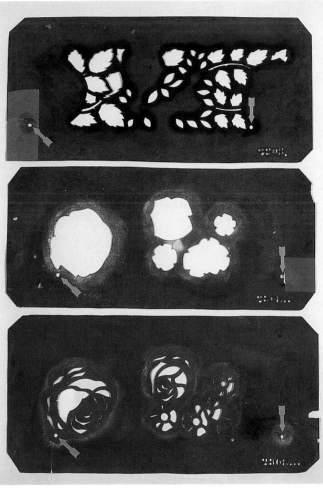

COLORS

Colors for the decoration are chosen to harmonize with the wall color and the room's furnishings. Since this cannot be judged by color harmony alone in the case of multicolored friezes, a sample should be prepared. Use a firm, smooth piece of cardboard. It should be about 1 millimeter thick so that it won't warp when painted. First paint on the background color and, after it dries, paint the decoration in the desired colors. The results can be a positive (or negative) surprise, for not only the color combination but also the shape of the design can have considerable influence on the overall effect. The cardboard should be big enough so that one can also make a second or third sample, and big enough to give an impression when one holds it on the wall and judges it for color.

Mixing Paint

This is primarily a matter of experience. If you don't feel confident mixing your own colors, you can work with the extensive array of prepared paints. Very nice results can be obtained with them. If you start out buying colors that come very close to your personal preferences, the job of mixing is reduced.

When the required amount is mixed but the desired color is not yet attained, use only a small amount of the paint to experiment further with, Otherwise you'll end up with too much. If you simply cannot come up with the desired color, it is simpler to start over. Remember, colors change as they dry, usually becoming lighter (though oil paints become darker). Therefore, only dried samples should be judged. Basically, the more you mix, the more grayish the results become. Since glaring colors are rarely wanted, a grayish tinge is not necessarily a bad feature.

These are only guidelines since everyone has their own preference in painting regarding thicker or thinner consistencies.

The quantity one needs is small. For a frieze 15 centimeters high and twenty meters long (to circle a room measuring five by four meters), 200 cubic centimeters of paint will suffice.

I advise you to mix a little extra of all the colors and use only part of them when painting on the walls. This way, if the pattern is damaged in some way, a laborious re-mixing won't be necessary. Besides, if one later decides to add something to the pattern, the right color will already be on hand and it won't need to be matched.

To get the right viscosity, mix poster or full-color paint with water at about a 1:1 ratio.

Colors for Striping

Striping as an accompaniment to a decoration is almost always suitable and can serve to separate wall and ceiling colors. As for suitable colors, use the same color as a single-color frieze, and for a multicolored one use any of the included colors or use the wall color, only a bit darker, or a contrasting color. Naturally, if you choose to use a color from the frieze for striping, it is necessary to mix somewhat more of it. The striping can be either a cover or a wash. Only a relatively thin, liquid paint can be used for neat lining, for it has to "run" well. If necessary, add some water—poster or full-tone paint can be thinned with water to a ratio of 1:3.

MARKING WITH A CHALK LINE

To begin with, determine at what height the decoration should run. Setting it directly under the ceiling may dull the effect. The general rule is to place it about a handbreadth below. The desired height is measured in each corner of the room and marked with a pencil. Since there are walls of unequal height, it may be necessary to vary the height by a couple centimeters.

It is important that the chalk lines meet in each corner at the same height! The chalk line is pulled out of its box, which is filled with a light powder (found in hardware and artist supply stores). Two people stretch the line from corner to corner and then one person reaches toward the center of the wall and pulls the line 20 to 30 centimeters away from the wall horizontally before letting it snap back. The snapped line leaves a straight line of chalk to serve as a guide.

This process is carried out on all the walls to be painted. On a very bumpy (old) wall, the line is stretched only moderately from corner to corner since it would not make its mark in the low spots otherwise.

This chalk line helps when applying the stencil and prevents the frieze from forming wavy lines. The chalk line can mark either the upper or lower edge of the decoration, with a corresponding line drawn in on the stencil. The stencil is then put on so that its marks match up with the chalk line.

If the decoration is to be accompanied by a stripe, then it is best to paint the stripe first and use this line to line up the stencil. In this case, the stripe must appear on the stencil where the stripe is wanted—thus at the right distance from the decoration (either above or below).

Since the chalk mixes with the paint when the stripe is painted, a light chalk color is recommended. It will not alter the paint color as much as dark chalk. To make this mixture as insignificant as possible, excess chalk should be blown away, or brushed off with a soft brush, before painting the stripe.

28. To keep the frieze level on the wall, one uses a chalk line, indicated by the number 1. The stripe on the pattern is lined up with the chalk line. The number 2 indicates completed stenciling; number 3 the stencil.

29. If the design is accompanied by a stripe, a chalk line is first made where the stripe goes. This line is used for locating and matches the stripe on the stencil. 1. Chalk line, 2. Stripe, 3. Stenciling, 4. Stencil with stripe.

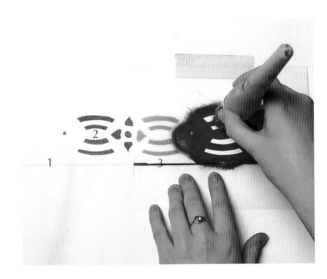

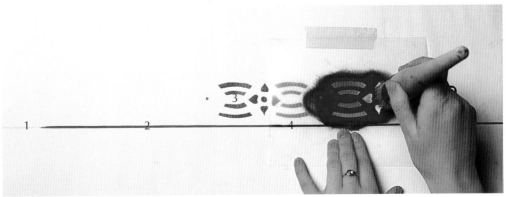

STRIPING

Striping is an almost indispensable style element. It looks elegant and offers many ways to decorate a wall or a corner nicely. Just a single line has an effect. Whether it runs over or under an decoration depends on whether the motif is standing or hanging.

For striping, one uses special wooden rulers with beveled edges. This prevents the paint from getting behind the ruler and messing up the wall. When striping, the beveled edge points toward the wall.

There is a special striping brush (see #18, 19) that is dipped into the paint only far enough to wet the bristles and then applied carefully—drawn along the ruler with a light touch until the paint runs out. Then the brush is dipped again and placed on the end of the stripe, where it became lighter, and the line is continued. Constant pressure must be applied to the striping brush, otherwise the line becomes heavier in some places, lighter in others. Use a little less pressure when first applying the brush because it still has a lot of paint in its bristles. Otherwise the line would become too heavy at the point of each new application. All of this sounds more complicated than it is, but it is still advisable to make several stripes on packing paper stuck to the wall, or on a practice card (see #18, no. 1), if you've never done this before. Getting a perfect continuation of the line through constant pressure and the right amount of paint on the bristles will soon become routine.

30. This large design is only suitable for corners of a room. Two stripes link the corner flowers.

31. Ceiling and wall design with stripes and bands.

32. Very elaborate painting with stripes of various widths and a marbled band on the ceiling and the window areas.

There are striping brushes in different sizes for lines of different widths. Very broad stripes, called bands, are painted by marking the upper and lower borders with chalk lines, painting over the lines with a striping brush, and then painting in the middle with a brush of appropriate width.

For the inexperienced, the following method is easier: Mark the edges of the band with chalk lines, put masking tape over them, paint, and remove the masking tape.

33. The wall color extends onto the ceiling, ending at the two stripes.

34. Part of the design shown on page 47 appears in each corner of the ceiling, linked with four stripes of different colors and widths for a very nice effect.

35. In striping, the wooden ruler defines the stripe with its beveled edge. One hand with spread fingers holds the ruler on the wall. The brush is held by its end and drawn lightly along the ruler until the paint runs out.

36. To paint a wide stripe or band, stripe the two edges along the chalk lines and paint in the center with a brush.

37. Another way to paint a band is to put masking tape along the chalk lines and paint between them with a brush, then remove the tape.

STENCILING

To avoid possible mistakes, practice. Just like with striping, use a practice card. There are four basic painting techniques to choose from; each with its own characteristics in terms of application and appearance.

Spotting to Cover

In dry spotting, the brush is dipped into the paint, wetting the tips of its bristles, and the excess paint is wiped off on cardboard. A test spot is made through the stencil. If the brush sticks too much, it is still too wet. The excess paint needs to be removed again. No paint is supposed to get behind the stencil. This test spotting should be done every time you wet the brush, even when one is already working on the wall. The feel for having the right amount of paint on the brush soon comes to you, but it can never replace wiping the brush and making at least one test.

After the test spotting, spot through the stencil until the paint appears to cover the area. This is especially important along the edges of the decoration. If the pattern has large surfaces (larger than the diameter of the brush), it makes sense to begin in the middle of the area. Should the brush still be too wet, then no harm will be done there, and it is as yet not too late to wipe it again.

I advise that you hold the stencil on the wall with a strip of masking tape. One hand holds the brush, the other presses the stencil onto the wall so it cannot slip. This also applies to the three following techniques.

Spotting to Wash

This is done in the same manner as described above, only less paint is applied, so that the background still shows through. The spotting paint may be somewhat thinner. In this technique, experience teaches you to achieve an even coat of paint.

Brushing

This method requires less expenditure of energy and less time but has other drawbacks: The striping, slightly turning brush movement can push paint behind the stencil if it does not lie flat, and if the brush holds even a little too much paint! It is done with a round brush equipped with longer and softer bristles. The decoration appears to be covered just as well as when spotted to cover—there is no visible difference.

Hatching

The two requirements for this method are a smooth surface and a decoration with a fairly large area. In hatching, the paint is applied with a paintbrush, which is only wet slightly at the ends, then drawn softly over the stencil so that the brush strokes can be seen.

It is very important to always wipe the brush in advance until it produces the desired brushstroke! One can paint in various directions, but don't apply too much since a washed appearance is desired. With this method, one must make sure that all the corners are painted. In this situation, the thinner the stencil, the more easily the corners and angles can be reached.

The surest method for the amateur is spotting to cover. The other three techniques require more sensitivity, which can be learned through practice.

When you practice spotting with cardboard, it can be seen at once whether the locating marks are in the right places. If not, then position the stencil again.

38. In stenciling by spotting, a round brush with short bristles is applied to the stenciled area with perpendicular, hammer-like motions, until the paint covers it.

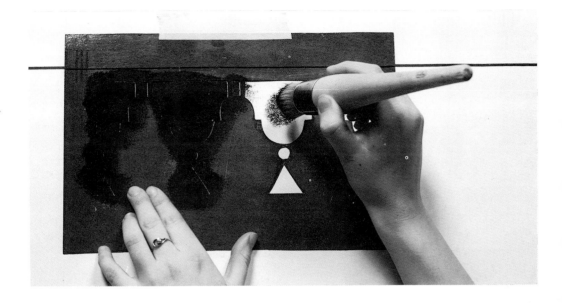

39. Stenciling by brushing: The round brush with long bristles is applied with a striping-circling motion. The stencil must be held on the wall very firmly.

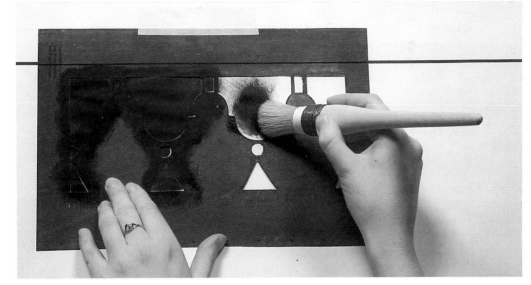

40. Stenciling by hatching: A wide paintbrush is moved gently across the stencil so the brush strokes can be seen. The paint is kept thin so the background color can be seen. Only the wash-like character makes the brush strokes visible.

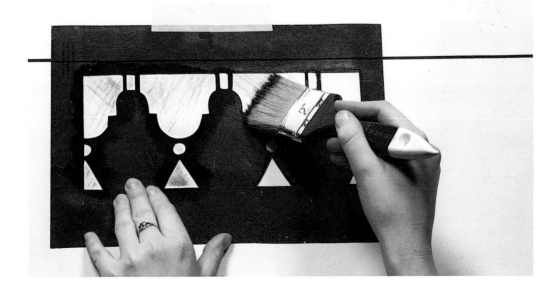

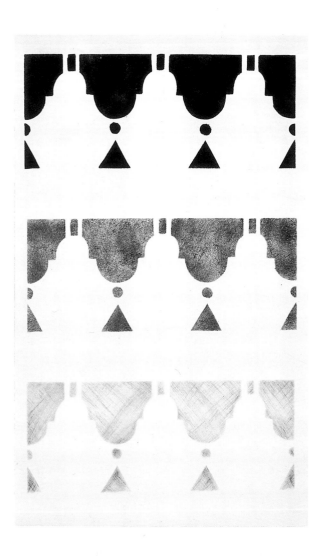

41. The three stenciling techniques demonstrated on the previous page are shown in their finished state—spotting to cover and brushing look the same in the top photo. In the center, spotting has been used to create an even, thin wash. The bottom photo shows the light brush strokes of hatching.

Spraying Methods

The four traditional brush techniques very quickly make one wonder whether spraying might not be quicker and more practical. Yet there are good reasons why these customary stenciling techniques have considerable advantages in enclosed spaces.

Toward the end of the 19th century, the spray gun was invented and used primarily for particular effects with negative stencils. This meant that the decoration was not cut out of the cardboard, but its outer contours were; thus it was not the decoration that appeared in color, but its surroundings. With the spray gun, the entire stencil was sprayed over, so that the contours appeared sharp and the transitions to the wall were soft and flowing. Covering the surroundings, as is necessary with the positive stencil, was completely omitted.

If one wanted to create the positive stencils shown in this book using spraying techniques (for example, airbrush), the stencils would have to have very wide borders, which would make them more difficult to handle. Or the surrounding area would have to be laboriously covered anew with every new position. Thus spray painting does not actually save any time, and requires additional adhesive material. And since most of the suitable paints contain poisonous solutions, enclosed spaces are not the right places to use them.

Also, spray painting equipment is expensive and requires a lot of experience to use. All in all, this technique is no alternative to brush painting. Even the inexpensive, easy-to-use spray paints readily available today are not desirable for this work because of the fumes they create.

STENCILING ON THE WALL

Stenciled Borders

For this work, a ladder is clearly impractical, since the materials cannot be put down on it and the radius of action is very limited. A table you can stand on works best.

The following materials should be on the table: the stencils, the stenciling paint, a plate into which to pour portions of the paint, masking tape, spotting brush, and cardboard on which to wipe off excess paint and test spot.

Striping, if included, can be done before or afterward from a ladder, though the table is more convenient. The ladder has to be moved too often. If the striping is also done from the table, then you need to add striping paint, a wooden ruler, and a striping brush to the materials.

Begin in the most inconspicuous corner of the room—this is where you end after going around the room, and here you have to accept the way the beginning and end match up if they do not match precisely, which is usually the case. The most inconspicuous place in the room is usually the corner to the right or left of the entrance door, or at a projecting (chimney) corner.

Measure to see how the pattern matches about five decoration lengths from the meeting point. With short decoration lengths it is much easier to solve problems than with long ones. If need be, fudge it. By stretching or reducing the gaps between the decorations, a few centimeters can be gained or lost. If that does not suffice, more extreme measures will be needed. This means leaving one part out of the decoration or adding one part to it. To do this, choose the part that can be manipulated most harmoniously. This fudging must not be too noticeable, for other than the "culprit," nobody should notice unless you confess.

With multicolored stencil designs, there are two possible methods: One can go around the room with each color, or complete the radius of action that you can reach from the table. In other words, paint the length of the table with the first color, then with the second, and so on. This is possible because the paint dries very quickly, so that within a short time one color can be added to another. In any case, the second method is recommended because the table does not have to be moved so often. If one is using more than one color, then one needs a brush for each one.

When you paint the first color, the locating marks must be painted too. For every succeeding color, they serve as sighting points for locating the stencil. With many stencils, they are painted their final color in the follow-up process. In such a (rare) case, the locating marks are always dots.

Corners that are hard to reach are naturally hard to paint. Cardboard stencils are easier to handle here, since they can be bent at right angles, whereas Mylar or Acetate curls. Particularly complicated designs can be omitted here and painted in freehand later. Finally, the inevitable drips are painted the color of the wall.

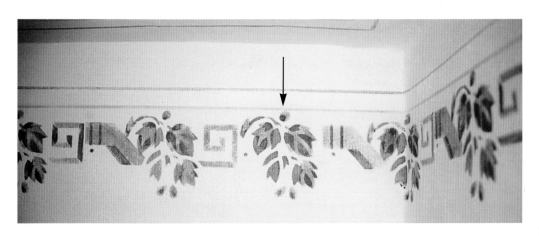

42. An example of a successful joint. Here the beginning and end meet. It is hard to see that the leaf (designated by an arrow) was painted at the wrong place.

43. A room with a wall-filling stencil design, frieze, stripes and single-color base. Redone like the original, which dated to about 1870.

WALL-FILLING STENCILS

Since these patterns are continued in all directions, one should again choose the most inconspicuous place to start .

Note: Over a door, the decoration is only 30 to 40 centimeters high, and has to be worked in as best one can over this short distance. Also, the job is much easier if you omit the corners. A stripe to the left and right of the corner will make this possible, and then every wall becomes an individual unit. The pattern ends at the stripe no matter where it is, which means that the job of holding the stencil in the corner is eliminated. The work process is as follows: make the vertical lines with masking tape, do the spot painting with the stencil, remove the masking tape, and paint the stripe.

In cases where the upper edge doesn't reach all the way to the ceiling, there are three ways to form the upper edge:

First, the decoration is "cut off" at the top, that is, bounded by a stripe. First mark off the upper edge, stick the stencil on, paint, remove the stencil, and stripe.

Second, cut off the top of the pattern and form the upper edge with a stripe and a frieze. First draw the lines, tape the stencil in place, paint, remove the stencil, paint the stripe, and paint the frieze between the stripes.

44/45. Above: a complete stencil design with four locating marks. Below: A surface with several of these designs. The triangle and lines show that the locating marks always form right angles.

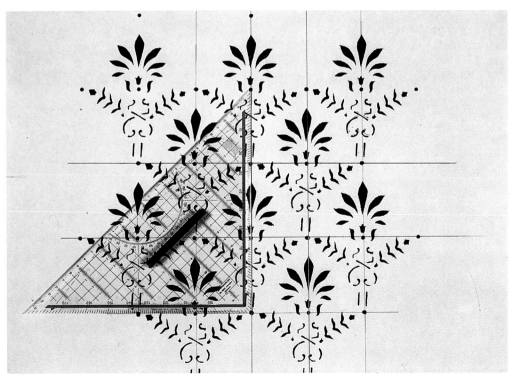

46. The corners can be left out of wall-filling designs when they are bordered by vertical lines. The photo shows a room of a house in Schwimbach before restoration. The decor was created between 1900 and 1910. Today the house is in the Franconian Open-air Museum in Bad Windsheim where it was rebuilt and restored.

47. Just as a frieze should never be directly under the ceiling, this wall-filling stencil design does not extend all the way up. A band and a stripe form its border.

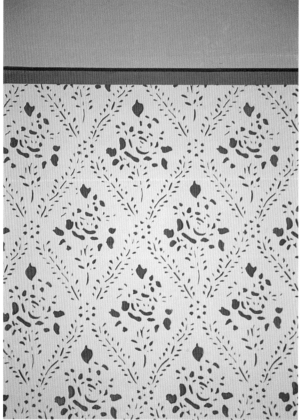

48. A frieze as upper border for a wall-filling design looks decorative and was the usual type of border. The photo shows a reconstruction of an original pattern in the original colors. The frieze is made with a negative stencil for the green background plus a positive stencil for the pink parts. The contours are created by the pale green wall color itself.

Third, the decoration does not go as high as the wall color but ends with the full pattern. First the upper row along the guideline is stenciled in, then one works downward. The ceiling and wall colors are separated by one or more stripes.

The lower end can go all the way to the floor or can stop sooner, at a baseboard. This is the most customary form. The baseboard is exposed to frequent damage. Thus it can be painted separately without having to renovate the whole room. In both cases, the decoration stops above it, however it looks best. A stripe between the baseboard and the wall pattern is obligatory. The baseboard can be the same color as the wall, but must be somewhat darker, or the color of the stenciled decor, if this is not lighter than the wall. Naturally, a contrasting color is also possible.

Stenciling an entire wall is, of course, very time consuming. Omitting corners, baseboards, and upper areas reduces the work. There is one more way to save time: This consists of stenciling only the baseboard. This has always been a very common option, especially for halls and stairways.

49. Another good upper border for a wall-filling stenciling: The wall color extends farther up than the painting, which ends with complete decorations and is not cut off as in the two previous examples. Note that the wall and ceiling colors are divided by a triple stripe using all three stencil colors. The picture shows a restored room in the Basket Museum in Michelau.

50. This can easily happen with a wall-filling decor: The designs extend too far (arrow) or are crowded too closely (circle).

51. This is a good way to decorate halls and stairways: Stenciling is only done on the lower walls. This wall was restored like the original. The white and dark blue colors on a gray-green background indicate that the original was made in the first decade of the twentieth century.

TIPS AND TRICKS

Despite precisely located markings, it is almost unavoidable that during the course of the work one goes off the vertical or horizontal line. Errors quickly add up when the positioning of the stencil goes awry, with the decorations running too close together or too far apart.

To avoid this problem, look at your work from a distance now and then. If you see that the design is going off track, correct it by adjusting the stencil appropriately for the next decoration. Don't correct the error completely in the next single decoration, but gradually over a greater area, bit by bit. This is less conspicuous. If a huge error has been made, there is nothing to do but paint over the mistakes with the wall color, let it dry, and paint the design again.

HARD-TO-REACH PLACES

These include the corners of the room and areas around door frames, radiators, and light switches. The switch panels can be unscrewed. To handle the corners of the room better, cut a stencil with just one decoration (with locating marks), or with only the necessary part of the decoration, since a small stencil is easier to handle. Corners are easier to paint with a thin, straight-cut bristle brush. It is simpler to use it around door frames too. One can also leave these areas out and cut the stencil to fit them at the end, to reach these areas better. Stenciling cannot be done behind radiators. Here the stencil has to be attached neatly on three or four sides and painted only as far as there is room to move the brush.

Scattered Patterns

Another possible way to decorate entire walls is with a scattered pattern. Since the pieces are not painted close together, this work takes considerably less time. The most suitable patterns are floral ones, which do not require one locating mark after another on the wall, but can be placed wherever you want. This means that the spotting paint does not have to cover the image. To give the flowers and leaves a natural and artistic character, spot painting combines covering and washing. In this manner, a single color sometimes appears lighter, sometimes darker, giving the flower a more three-dimensional look. Several colors, gently blending into each other in the decoration, enhance the artistic effect. The decoration in #53 shows flowers spot painted in this manner. The individual leaves and blossoms are very suitable for a scattered pattern. Other well-suited scattered patterns can be made with stencils of parts of the design.

After floral patterns, strictly graphic contours are also suitable if they sometimes appear on the wall complete and sometimes only in part. For this, spot paint either to cover or to wash, but not both at once as with the flowers. One color or more is a matter of personal taste. If the colors of drapes, furniture or floor are repeated in the wall pattern, the room takes on a harmonious overall appearance. For a graphic scatter pattern, a design such as that in #52 can be used.

52. A two-colored stencil (also on page 49) in white and blue forms a frieze on a gray-blue background. Beneath it, individual decorations are scattered at will.

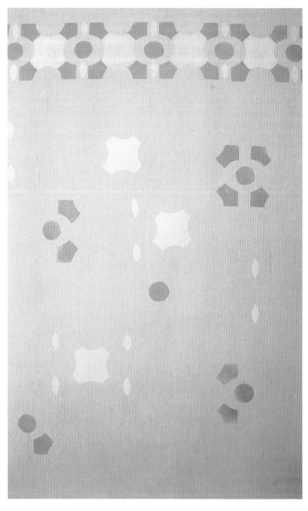

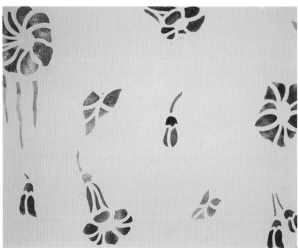

53. The stencil design from Page 65 is used for a scattered pattern. The stencil for the leaves is painted in two-tone green and that of the flowers in red and blue.

SPATTERING

In spattering, the entire wall is sprayed with one or more colors. It is done with a coarse push broom, dipping the bristles into paint and then bending them back by hand so that when released they spatter the paint on the wall (#54). (No matter what, cover the floor before you start spattering.) The drops of paint will be of different sizes. For more than one color, apply them one after the other (not mixed). Whether the spattering extends over the stenciling or just decorates the wall beneath it or the entire background is a matter of personal taste. It can also be done as an independent design without a frieze.

Spattering can also be created through other methods, for example, with a toothbrush. The bristles, like those of the push broom, are bent backward with your fingers and then released, spattering very small spots on the wall. The paint has about the same viscosity as striping paint—almost watery. Somewhat larger spots can be made with a paintbrush. It is dipped into paint and struck against a stick or a brush handle so that the spots land on the wall. Spotting with a toothbrush or paintbrush takes somewhat longer than using a big push broom, but it provides a better appearance. The time required also depends on the desired quantity of spots.

54. A coarse push broom is dipped in paint and used for spattering the wall. One pulls the bristles backward, toward oneself, and then lets them go, spattering the wall with drops of paint.

55. Here the gray and yellow background and frieze have been spattered with black and white spots.

56. A strip of black spots separates the wall and ceiling colors. The roses and background are spattered with small gray spots. Such small spots are created using a toothbrush.

SPONGE SPOTTING

Like spattering, sponge spotting creates a background. It is attractive enough to be used alone, without a frieze. Using a tone similar to that of the background avoids contrasts that are too crass. The whole wall can be painted this way, and a frieze looks good on a sponge-spotted wall, or the sponge spotting can stop at a border. The same consistency of paint used for brush spotting is suitable for sponge spotting (see page 18). On a plate or can lid, dip a dampened natural sponge (from the drugstore) into the paint and squeezed it out well, otherwise there will be blurs instead of gentle traces of the sponge. Spot the sponge on the wall with light pressure and keep turning it to avoid a repeating pattern. The sponge has many "faces" on its surface and can provide a changeable pattern.

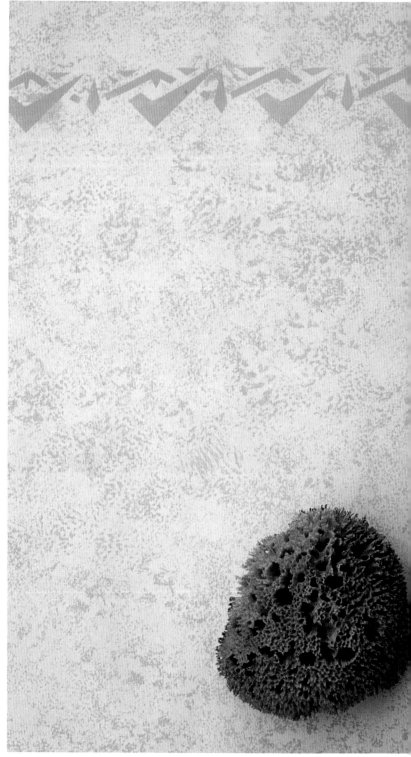

57. This natural sponge created this lively background; then a stenciled pattern was applied in the same color (shown somewhat larger on Page 117).

DECORATING WITH METAL FOIL

Metal foil can be bought at an art supply shop or directly from a gold-leaf factory as gold, silver, brass, aluminum, or copper foils. Since working with genuine gold or silver foil requires some experience as well as expensive, special tools, this chapter is limited to the less-expensive brass and aluminum foils. The latter has the advantage of not oxidizing (as silver does). Both of these foils, as well as copper foil, are best suited for use on walls.

One begins as follows: When the frieze is painted, the parts that are to be done in metal are covered with white glue, using a fine-pointed paintbrush. The white glue is the adhesive. It is applied in a thin but covering coat. After fifteen minutes, or when the milky liquid has become clear, the metal is applied. The metal sheets are divided by hand into pieces of the right size, laid flat, and pressed with wadding. The projecting edges are bent back with a soft brush.

If there are gaps after the work is done, then apply more glue and metal using the same process.

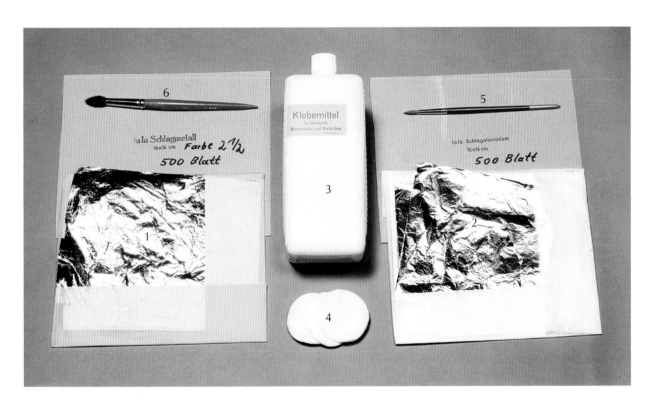

58. Tools and materials for metal foil work:
1. Metal foil (brass)
2. Aluminum foil
3. Glue
4. Wadding
5. Pointed brush for glue
6. Brush to use on foil edges.

59. First the surface to be gilded is covered with white glue and allowed to dry until the glue turns clear.

60. An appropriate-size piece of foil can be created using your hands.

61. Place the foil on the glued area after the glue is almost dry).

62. Press foil on using wadding.

63. Push back excess foil with the brush, called "turning in."

64. Once the foil decoration is completed, a black rim remains around the gold to keep it from blending into the background.

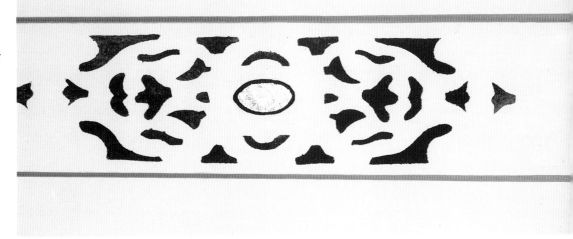

Part II
DECORATIONS

SINGLE-COLOR STENCILS

65. A brown border creates a striking contrast on a beige wall, with a red stripe below and a brown one above. The floral motif is just as usable for a two-colored design if it is divided into two stencils.

66. Four patterns with small designs. The third from the top (red on a light blue background) has been matched to its original colors.

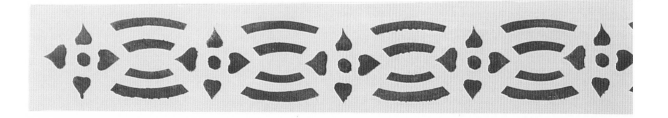

67. The colors of the top and bottom borders match the original ones. In the second design, one can paint every third rose white. The rose pattern at the bottom was placed about 1.7 meters high above a lilac base.

68/69. Two color schemes for the same motif.

70. A very elaborate, single-color floral border, painted in bright blue on a pale blue background. ↓

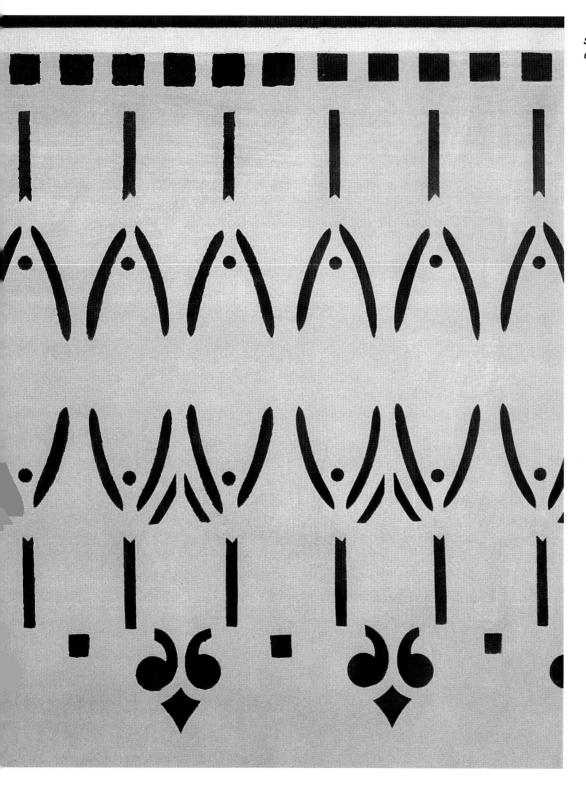

71. This large motif, looks soft thanks to its airy, netlike character.

72. This pattern creates a lace curtain effect, with white on a pale green background.

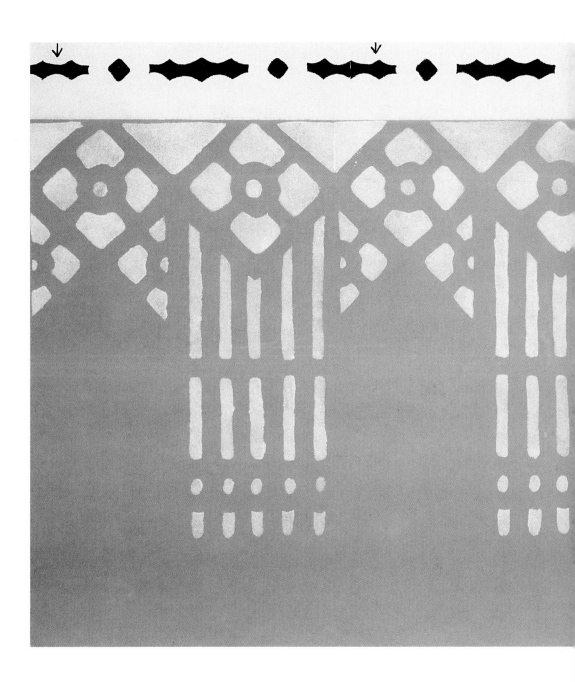

73. The vivid blue on a yellow background was matched to the original.

74. First designed as a single-color stencil, this has been done in two colors.

75. The light blue on a pale gray background matches the original.

76. A single-color stencil spotted in three colors.

77. This design is shown in its original form on Page 11.

78. This design was used to decorate the kitchen shown on pages 106-107. The small dark dots are grains of sand in the whitewash.

79. *This gentle motif was found on molding, as shown in #2, Page 6, and was used in a hall, pictured in #51, Page 31.*

MULTICOLOR
STENCILS

80. This stencil is located above white tiles. First the green was painted, then the blue. Parts of the design serve as locating marks.

81. The second color, red, partly overlaps the first color, blue.

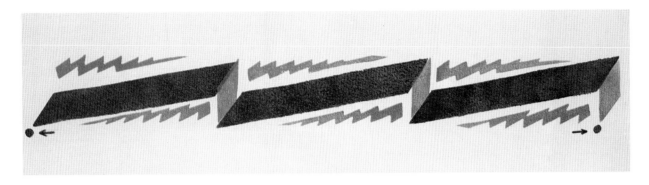

82. Here the locating marks
are blue dots that can be painted
over with the wall color afterward.

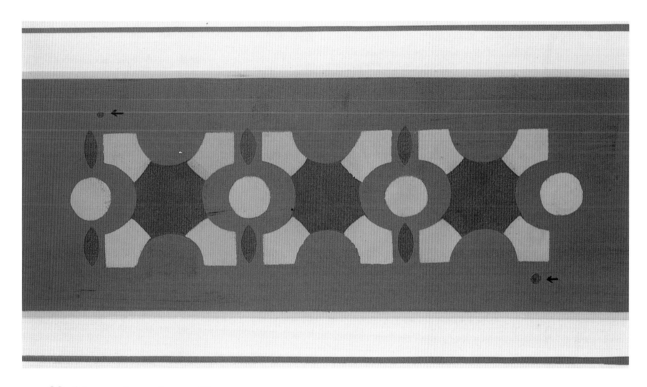

83. A two-color pattern with
four stripes on a band. Another
possibility for this motif is shown
on Page 32.

84. The first color is blue, the
second red, the third yellow. The
locating marks were painted
over later with the wall color.

85. The first color is pink, the second purple, with a pink stripe.

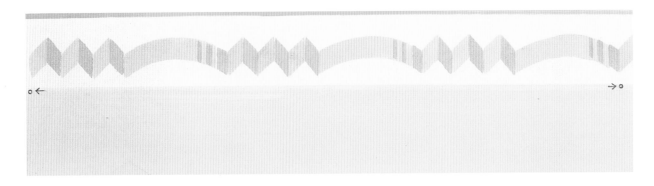

86. A yellow wall with a pulled-down white ceiling color are adorned with this simple stencil made first from the yellow wall color followed by a darker yellow. The locating marks were painted over.

87. For this stencil, the first color is gray, the second yellow, the third green. The locating marks can be painted over, or the gray dots can be used as locating marks.

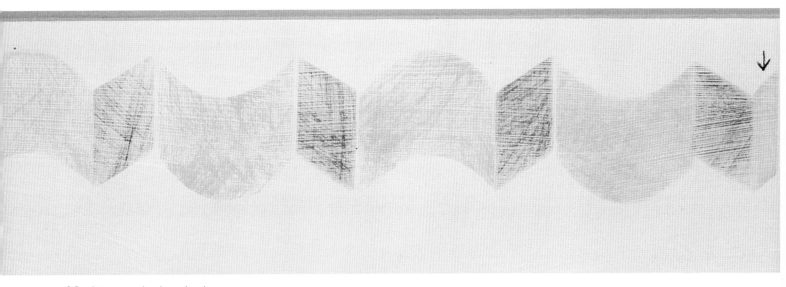

88. A two-color hatched
motif. Either gray or green can
be painted first.

89. First color red, second
gray.

90. Above: first color gray, second blue. Below: first color gray, second red, sometimes overlapping.

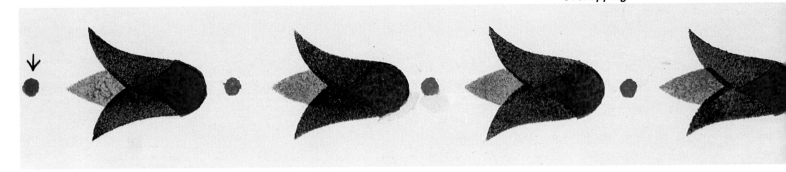

91. First color green, second blue, third red. The dots are painted the first color as locating marks, but get their final color—here red—with the final painting.

92. First color gray, second
medium blue, third dark blue.
The dots get their final color
with the third painting.

93. First color turquoise,
second blue. The turquoise dots
are painted over in blue.

94. First color blue, second red.

95. First color green, second gray, on a pale green wall. The locating marks are painted over.

96. Here the red spots of the flowers are the locating marks. Red is painted first, then gray and green in either order.

97. This gray band allows the flowers to be painted white—the white petals are locating marks. The centers of the flowers were later painted orange and yellow with a brush.

98. First color red, second
gray, with red stripe.

99. First color dark green,
painted rather like a wash,
second light green.

100. Three-colored overlapping pattern, first color dark blue, second medium blue, third light blue. The three are shown individually on Page 12.

101. Garland with stripe, original is shown on Page 6.

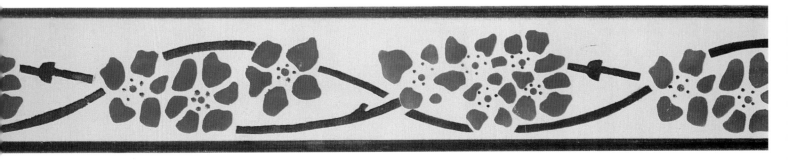

102. Floral border with stripes; design parts are locating marks.

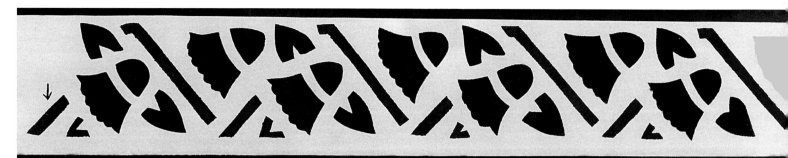

*103. This two-color stencil
between two stripes uses the
design parts as locating marks.*

*104. Three-colored
garland with black stripe is
shown in original colors.*

105. First color light, second dark. The locating marks are painted over.

106. Three multicolored forms of this stencil are shown on Page 7. Part of the design provides locating marks.

107/108/109. In these three floral-motif friezes with stripes, the leaves are always painted first for locating marks.

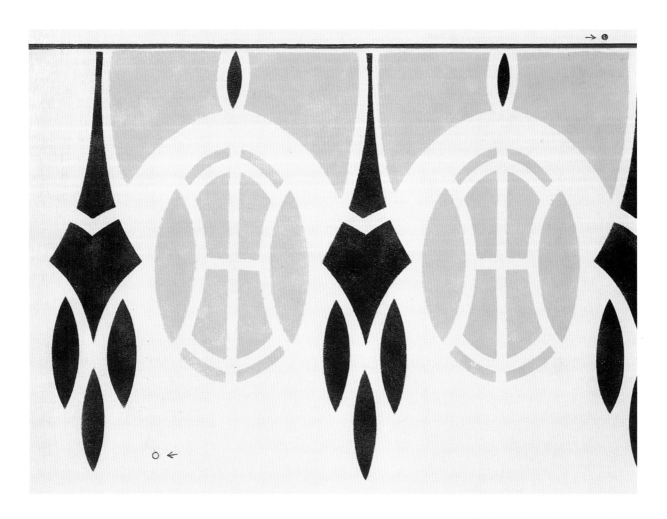

110. Here the stripe over the design is dominant, as the motif is "hung on it." The dots are painted over.

111. A two-colored design, but instead of making a second stencil for the second color, one can simply turn the first one over.

112. The original colors were white and dark blue on a gray-green background. Above it, the white ceiling color is pulled down to a dark blue dividing stripe above the wall color.

113/114. Two floral motifs in which the locating marks are painted over. In the lower flower, green is painted on yellow.

115. The locating marks are
part of the motif. Two interpre-
tations of these flowers are
shown on pages 32 and 102.

MULTICOLOR STENCILS WITH SHAPED DRAWINGS

You can make your own stencils using these drawings: Photocopy the drawing, fill in the outlines in various colors (as shown here in the book), or use a color copier. Transfer every color individually onto Mylar or Acetate or cardboard and cut it out. Remember to cut out the outlines of the drawings, or else the ornamental parts will be made smaller.

I suggest that you shade in all the areas to be cut out. This makes the areas easier to see. And don't forget to cut out the locating marks in every stencil too!

The colors of the drawings indicate:
Black: first coat
Red: second coat
Blue: third coat
Green: fourth coat
Purple: fifth coat

116/117. A two-colored design. The drawing shows one design, the frieze two; both are hatched with the same green. Where the stencils overlap, the green looks darker. The wash-like character lets the design look light and airy. The room on page 108 was painted with this stencil.

118/119. *A three-colored design. The drawing shows one design, the frieze shows the pattern repeated. Colors painted over another should be relatively thick so they cover.*

*122/123. A
three-colored design.
Each picture shows one
design.*

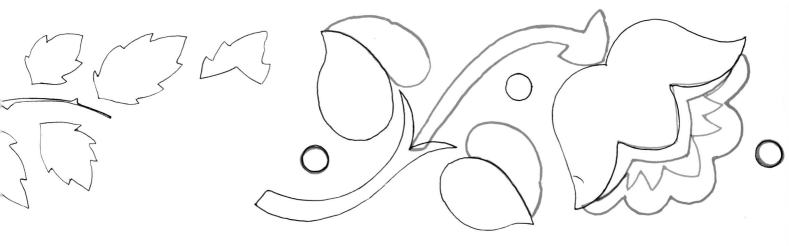

124/125. A three-colored design. The drawing shows one design, the frieze three, used as a decorative border over white tiles.

126/127. A two-colored design, each picture showing one design.

128/129. A three-colored design, the drawing showing one design, the frieze two.

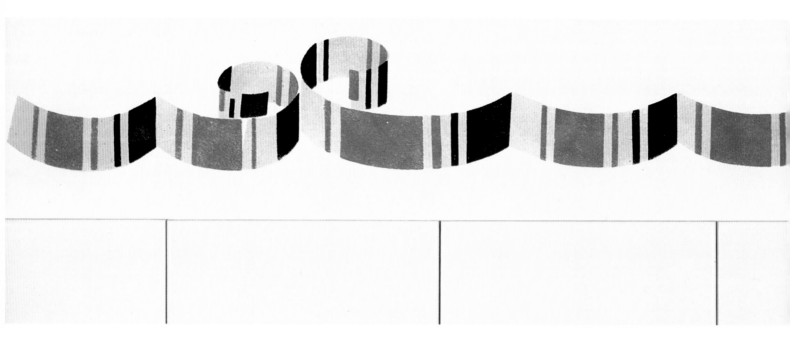

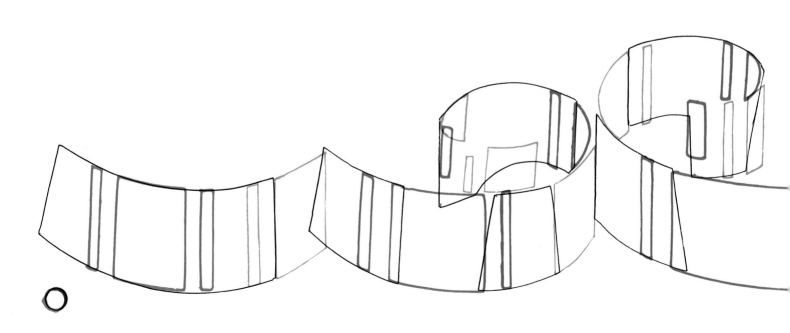

132/133. A three-colored design. The drawing shows the design, the frieze shows it repeated twice.

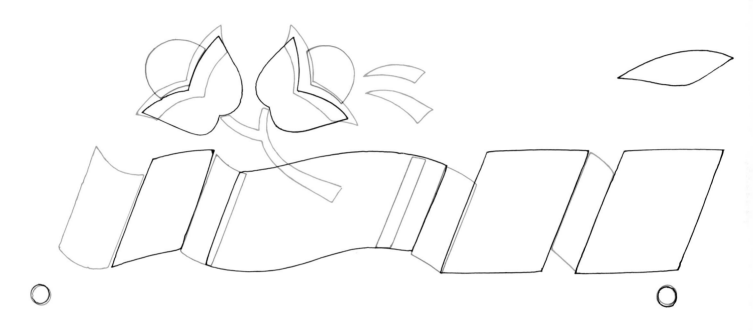

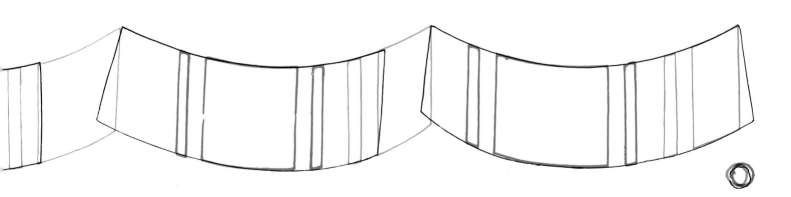

134/135. A three-colored
design, each picture showing one
design. The bellflower at lower
right can also be used as a
separate border, as on Page 52.

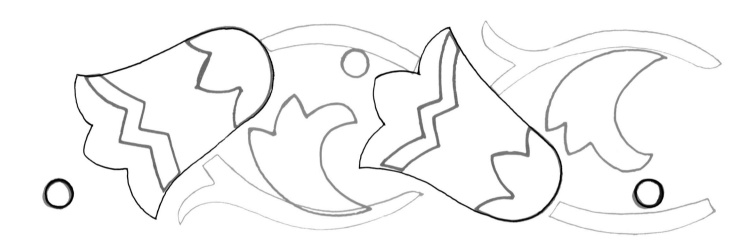

136/137/138.
*A four-colored
design, the
drawing
shows one design,
the friezes two,
with two color
combinations.*

139/140. A three-colored design with metal foil decoration. The drawing shows one design, the frieze two.

*141/142. A
five-colored
design, the
drawing showing
one design, the
frieze two.*

143/144. A
four-colored
design, the
drawing showing
one design, the
frieze two. Note,
the red-outlined
second color in
the drawing was
turned into two
colors in the
frieze— yellow on
the flowers and
green on the
leaves.

147/148/149. A five-colored design, the drawing showing one design, the frieze two. The upper drawing includes colors 1, 2 and 3, the lower one 4 and 5.

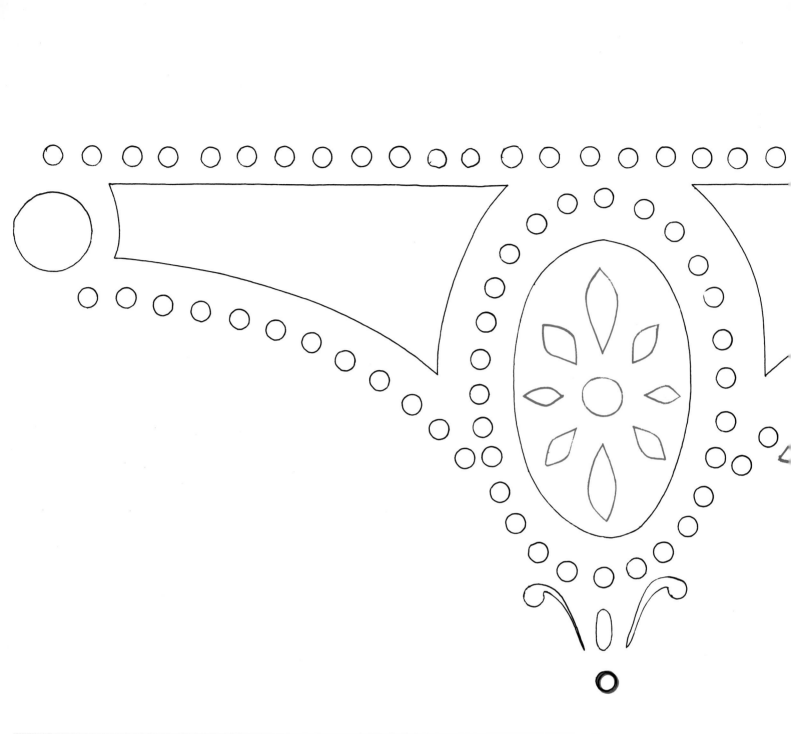

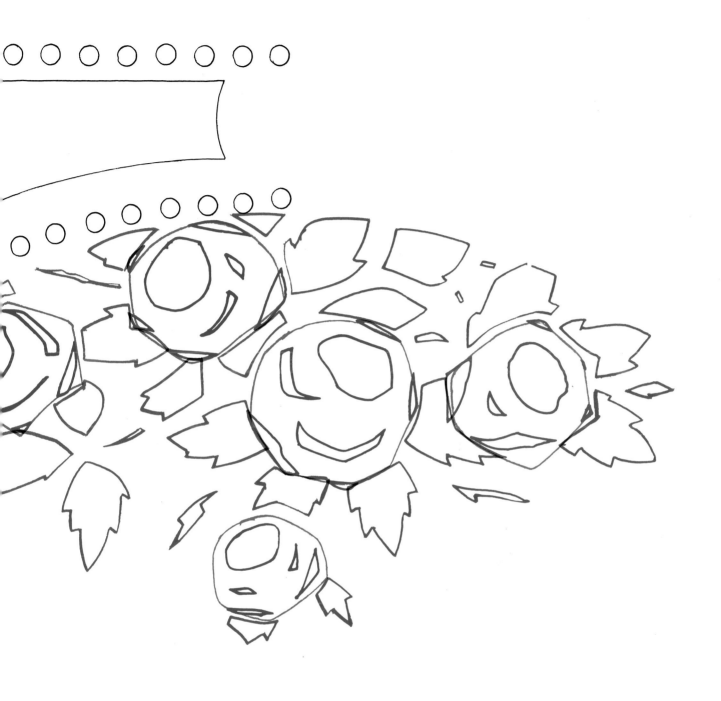

150/151. A four-colored design, the drawing showing one design, the frieze two. Note: The third color (blue outline) was painted yellow on the flowers and green in the oval.

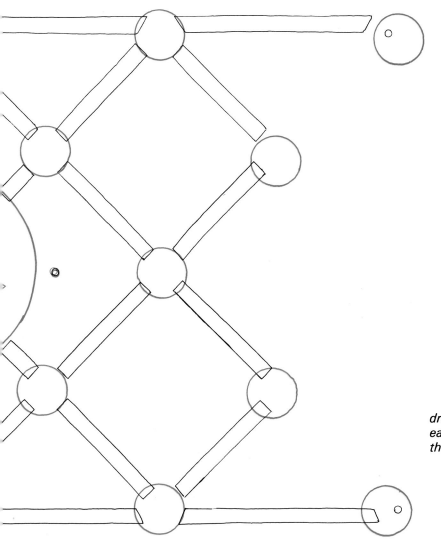

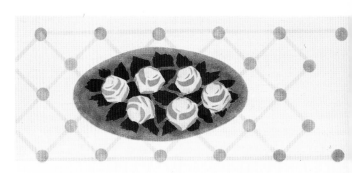

152/153/154/155. A five-colored design, the drawings and colored pictures showing one design each. The upper drawing includes colors 1, 2, and 3, the lower 4 and 5.

STENCILS WITH
METAL FOIL DECORATION

156. First color white, second blue. Which parts are done in foil is up to one's personal taste.

157. First color gray, second blue, with gold stripes.

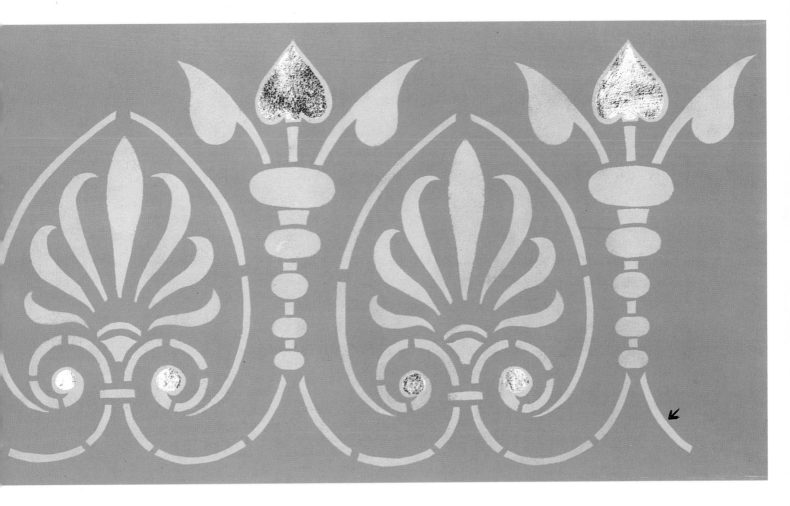

158. This design was found placed on a concave molding. The original colors were brown and gray; see #2, page 6.

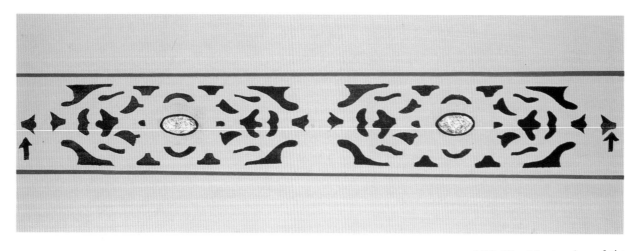

159. The black edge of the oval surrounds the gold so it does not disappear into the background.

160. The earthy colors and the gold go well with the antique wave motif. The waves are stenciled on a band.

161. A drawing for this five-color stencil is on Page 80.

162. A drawing for this three-color stencil is shown on Page 79.

DECORATIONS FOR WALL-FILLING STENCILING

163. Colored as in the original. The hatching shows the pattern. Three locating marks are outside it.

164. This wall decoration is shown in its original colors. The hatched area shows the pattern. There are two locating marks inside and one outside the hatching. The picture shows a wall decoration with two borders as upper closings. The cream ceiling color is pulled down to the wall.

165. *Original colors. The hatching shows the pattern, with one locating mark inside and four more outside it.*

166. *Original colors, plus the irregular rows of dots. Since the pattern is very small, the stencil can include several repeats.*

*167. Original colors, with a
clever frog frieze.*

168. Here two different stencil patterns were combined without division. Page 110 shows a room reconstructed with this motif. See #3, Page 6 for original colors.

169. The hatched area shows
the pattern, with two locating
marks inside it and four outside.
See #3, Page 6 for original
colors.

170. The hatching shows the pattern, with two locating marks inside it and two outside.

DECORATED SPACES

171. Here the stencil from Page 66 was used, with two narrow stripes added.

172. The single-color stencil shown on Page 120 was done here in three colors. Two gray spots from the first painting are repeated in the red and green paint as holes for the locating marks. The beginning forms the center over the window, from which stencils, mirror images of each other (clean the stencil and turn it over), lead left and right and down the sides.

173. Here the two-colored design shown on Page 69 is placed by itself as a crown for the doorway. The left and right outer parts of the light blue were omitted.

174/175. This black stenciling on a rough white background suits this kitchen. A few small design parts are done in gold and silver metal foil. Since the Art Nouveau motif, 31 centimeters high, is too big to be lined up in a room 2.5 meters high, the long blocks were put at some distance from each other. Stencil on page 10.

176. This 33-centimeter flower motif is too big for a room 2.5 meters high. Used only in the corners, in mirror images, and linked with stripes, it loses its luxuriance. On the right-hand side, the darker flower parts were spotted in two colors, creating an airy, artistic effect. All the blossom and plant parts are suitable for blended colors. Stencil on page 65.

177/178/179. Guests often compliment the two-color stenciling decorating the dining room of this inn. The room decor is crowned by the repetition of the wall frieze on the capital of the pillar. Since there was not enough space for the complete decoration over the window, only the upper part was continued, a solution that looks very natural. The stripe above the design is striking with the frieze is hung from it.

180. This palm-like pattern was found while clearing a ceiling. Every third design was gilded in the center. Stencil on page 122.

181. A small, rural kitchen is decorated with a single-color floral border. See stencil on pages 122-123.

182. The cloudy gray decoration is intended to harmonize with the marble. It's the same motif pictured below.

183. This frieze was reconstructed just as it was found in this same room (see stencil on Page 24).

184/185. The frieze and color are the same as the original in this authentic restoration. This kitchen shows how timely and esthetic historical room decor can be today. Stencil on Page 46.

186. Three other variations
of this floral border are shown
on Page 7. The stripe runs
underneath this standing decoration. Stencil on page 59.

187. In this two-color stenciling (see also Page 99), the two coats were spotted like a wash with the same green shade. The special effect created by the overlapping stencil is the darker green of the twice-painted areas. Thus the overall effect is of a two-tone design. This effect can only be created with overlapping, wash-spotted stenciling. The red and green stripes are above the decoration, which has a hanging character. Stencil on Page 66.

188. The flower motif in this frieze was chosen to echo the flowers in the two stove tiles, both Art Nouveau style. The flower pattern was found in an original design. The original colors of red and green were not used, but replaced by green, yellow and rust red for the flowers. Stencil on Page 13.

189/190. A room reconstructed in its original pattern (see #3, Page 6). The two decorations were used without being separated by a stripe. The upper one grows naturally out of the lower one.

SINGLE-COLOR STENCILS IN BLACK AND WHITE

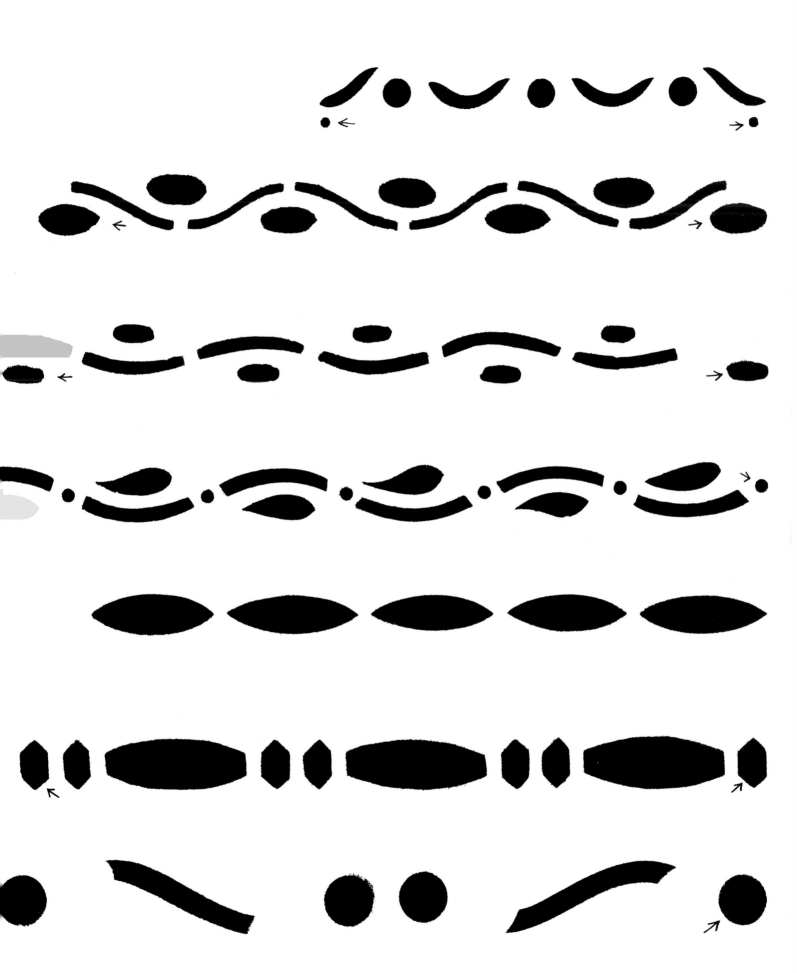

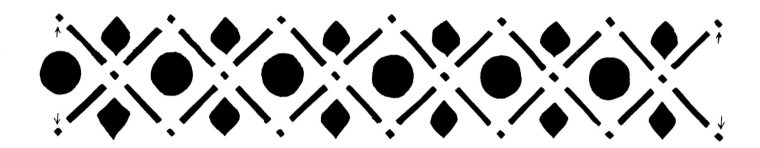

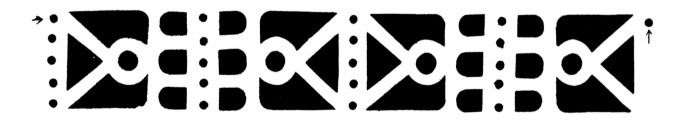

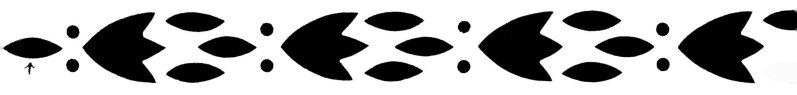

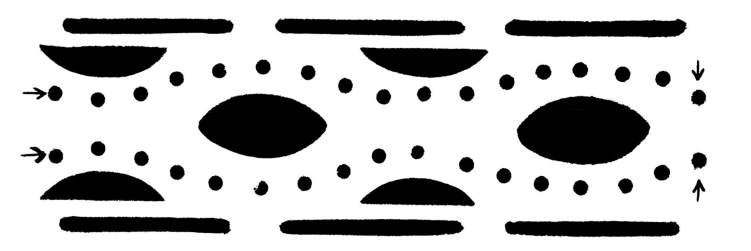

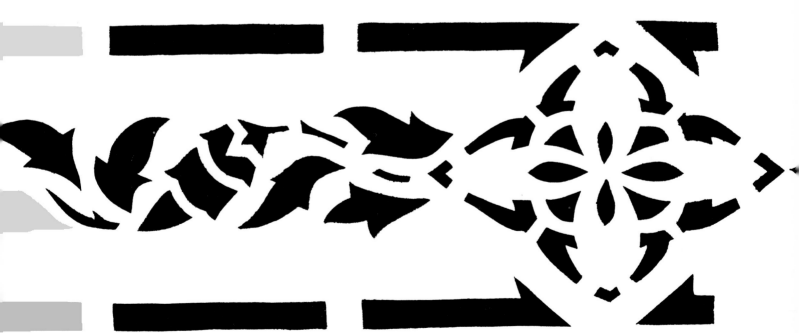

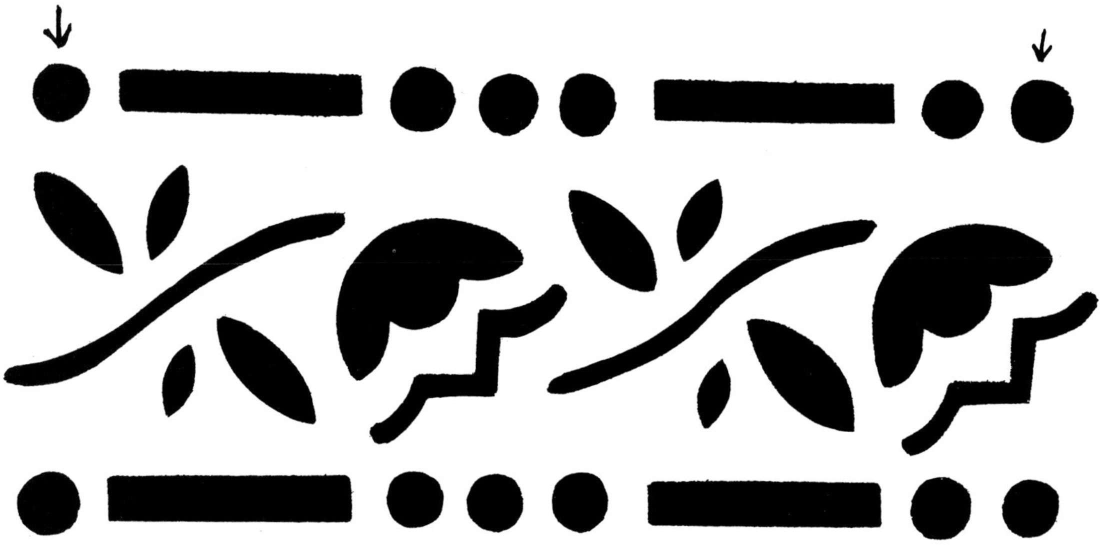

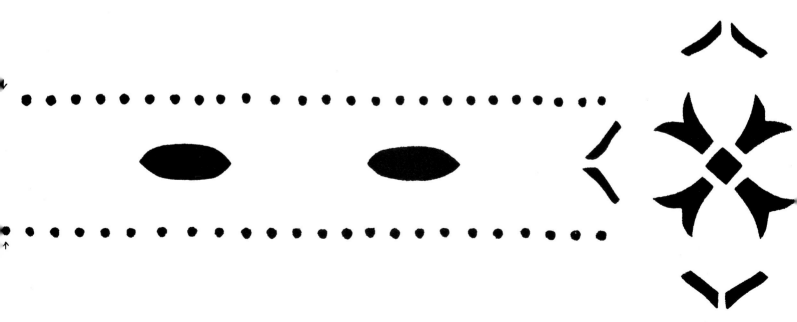